BOOK THREE

HAL LEONARD
GUITAR
TAB METHOD

Written by Michael Mueller

Contributing Editors: Kurt Plahna and Jeff Schroedl

To access audio visit:
www.halleonard.com/mylibrary

Enter Code
3112-2314-5815-7081

ISBN 978-1-4803-8734-8

HAL•LEONARD® CORPORATION
7777 W. BLUEMOUND RD. P.O. BOX 13819 MILWAUKEE, WI 53213

Visit Hal Leonard Online at
www.halleonard.com

BARRE CHORDS

In Book One, you learned basic open chords and movable power chords. Now it's time to put those two concepts together. A **barre chord** is really just a movable open chord, where your index finger lies flat across all six strings and functions as the nut, while your remaining three fingers fret the required notes.

E-SHAPE MAJOR BARRE CHORDS

The most common is the movable E chord shape. Form an open E chord by fretting the 5th, 4th, and 3rd strings with your ring, pinky, and middle fingers, respectively. Then slide those three fingers up one fret and lay your index finger across all six strings. The result is an F chord. Check out the **chord diagrams** below, which are graphic representations of the fretboard often used in guitar notation.

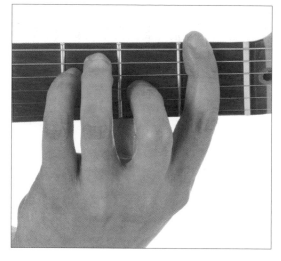

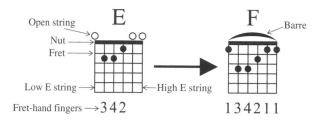

The root of the E-shape barre chord is on the 6th string. If you play this shape at the 3rd fret, you're playing a G major barre chord.

WALK DON'T RUN

This Ventures surf tune is best known for its guitar melody, but the rhythm guitar part is a great introduction to barre chords.

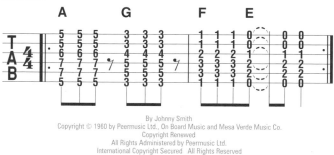

BABA O'RILEY

Get started with barre chords by playing this variation of the Who's classic riff.

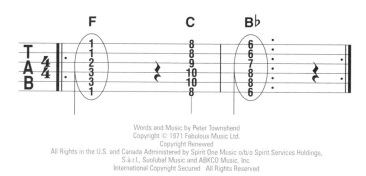

ARE YOU GONNA BE MY GIRL

Jet hit cruising altitude with this 2003 hit, which is also a nod to Iggy Pop's 1977 hit "Lust for Life." For the **double-stop bend** (bending two notes at once), make a small barre with your ring finger across strings 2 and 3.

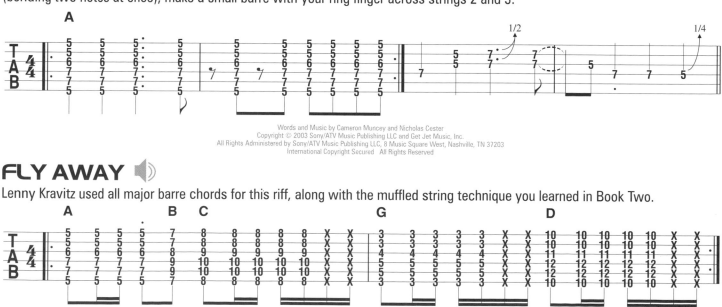

FLY AWAY

Lenny Kravitz used all major barre chords for this riff, along with the muffled string technique you learned in Book Two.

E-SHAPE MINOR BARRE CHORDS

To play the minor barre chord, fret the E-shape barre chord and then lift your middle finger off the 3rd string. The result is a movable version of an open Em chord.

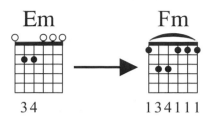

DRIVE MY CAR

Play barre chords in a driving quarter-note rhythm for the chorus of this Beatles hit.

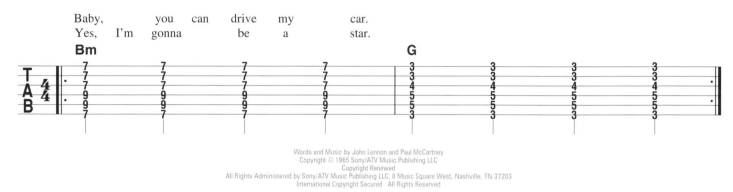

ALL ALONG THE WATCHTOWER

Jimi Hendrix's definitive cover of this Bob Dylan classic makes use of both minor and major forms of the E-shape barre chord.

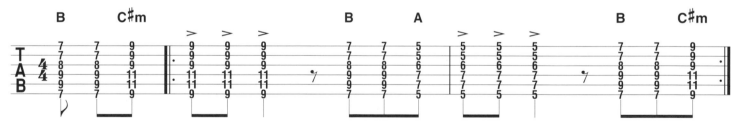

GO YOUR OWN WAY

Written by Lindsey Buckingham, "Go Your Own Way" was the first single from Fleetwood Mac's monumental 1977 release, *Rumours*.

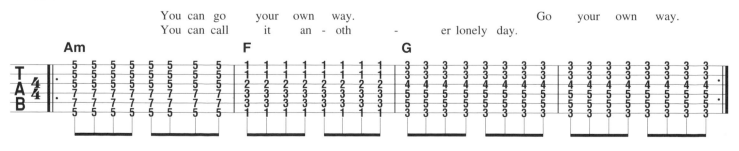

OH, PRETTY WOMAN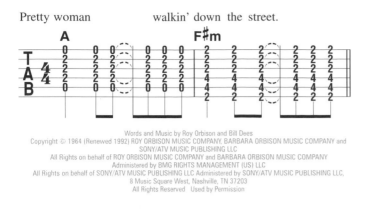

The verse of this timeless classic requires you to change between open chords and a minor barre chord.

REFUGEE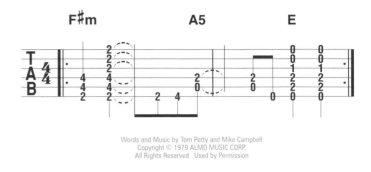

This early Tom Petty hit features the F#m barre chord in its main riff.

FOR YOUR LOVE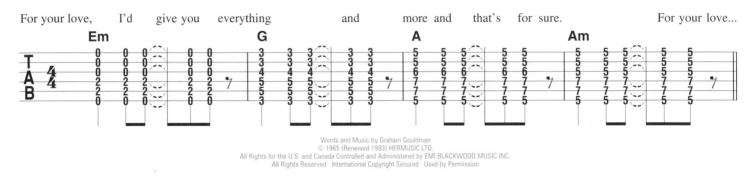

The intro, verse, and chorus of this Yardbirds classic features a cool shift from A major to A minor.

TWO PRINCES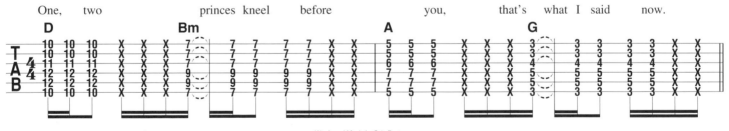

The major and minor barre chords are the easy part of this Spin Doctors track. Navigating the syncopated rhythm is a bit tougher, so review your sixteenth notes and rests.

HEAT OF THE MOMENT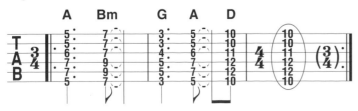

Progressive rockers Asia employed a changing time signature in this riff.

MY FAVORITE MISTAKE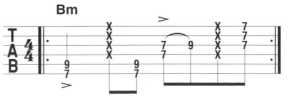

A minor barre chord mixed with muffled strings and a hammer-on sets up a catchy groove in this Sheryl Crow song.

CRAZY ON YOU

This iconic riff from Heart contains a very fast switch from an open Am to an F barre chord. This is a true test of your barre chord chops.

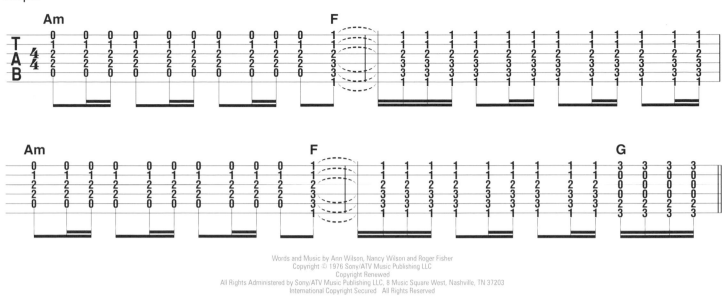

ALL I HAVE TO DO IS DREAM

For the F#7 chord in the bridge of this Everly Brothers hit, play an F# major barre chord and lift your pinky finger off the 4th string. Just like the E-shape major and minor chords you've learned, notice how this E-shape dominant seventh barre chord resembles the open E7 chord.

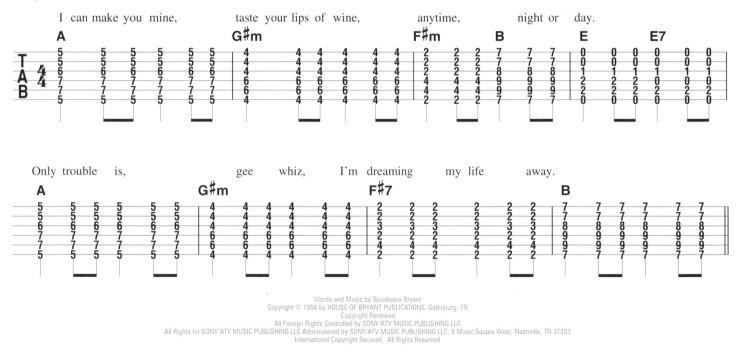

STAIRWAY TO HEAVEN

There are quite a few standout sections in Led Zeppelin's magnum opus, and the bridge following the solo is certainly one of them.

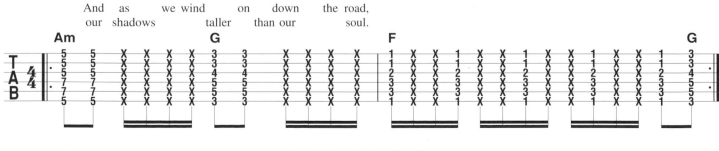

A-SHAPE MAJOR BARRE CHORDS

The next most common barre chord is the movable A chord shape. It is sort of a "double barre" chord, in that you need to barre strings 4–2 with your fret hand's ring finger, while your index finger barres both the 5th and 1st strings (the 6th string is not played).

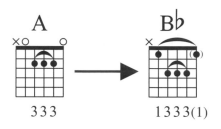

The fretted note on the high E string is often left out of the chord. You should be able to play it with or without it. Alternatively, you can also fret this shape using fingers 2, 3, and 4 on strings 4–2, while still barring with the index finger. Also, note that the root of the A-shape barre chord is on the 5th string, so if you play it at the 3rd fret, you're playing a C major barre chord.

COCAINE

The main riff of this Clapton classic comprises just two A-shape major barre chords: E and D.

LIVING AFTER MIDNIGHT

Judas Priest may be best known for power-chord riffs, but they used full-on major versions for this heavy metal hit.

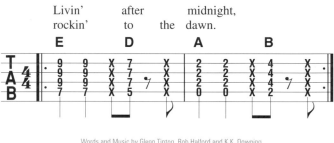

AMERICAN WOMAN

The Guess Who used A-shape major barre chords exclusively for their most famous song, "American Woman."

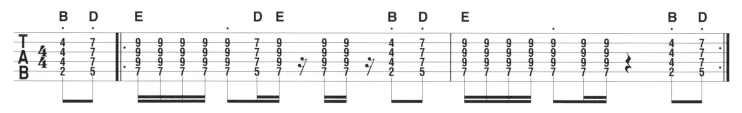

EVIL WAYS

Santana used this popular Latin progression in their 1967 hit.

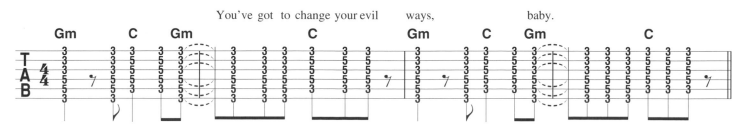

A-SHAPE MINOR BARRE CHORDS

To play the minor version of the A-shape barre chord, fret an open Am chord using your ring, pinky, and middle fingers on the 4th, 3rd, and 2nd strings, respectively. Then slide the chord up one fret and lay your index finger across the top five strings.

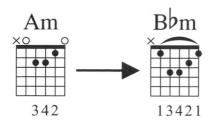

ANOTHER ONE BITES THE DUST

Queen's Brian May showed off his funk chops with this classic Em scratch riff.

How do you think   I'm gonna get a - long   with - out you when you're gone?   You
took me   for everything   that I   had   and   kicked me out   on my own.

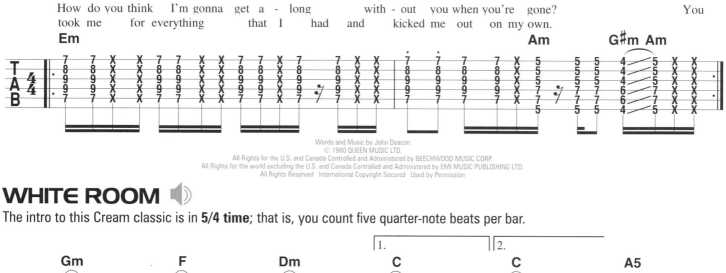

WHITE ROOM

The intro to this Cream classic is in **5/4 time**; that is, you count five quarter-note beats per bar.

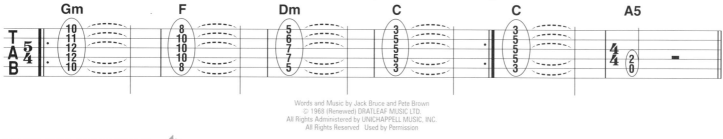

KRYPTONITE

3 Doors Down found superhuman staying power with its 2000 hit "Kryptonite," which features this modern **arpeggio** (broken chord) riff.

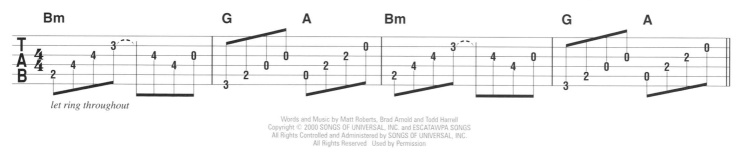

let ring throughout

SULTANS OF SWING

Mark Knopfler's two guitar solos are widely regarded among the greatest in rock history, but the verse's simplicity is the song's backbone.

You get a shiver in the dark,   it's   raining   in the park, but meantime,
          south of the river   you stop   and you hold   everything.

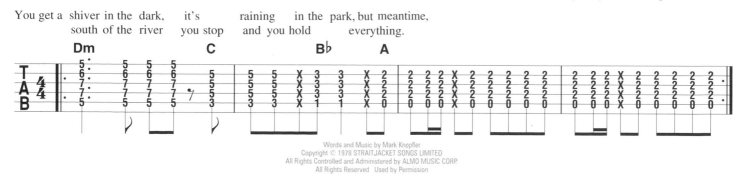

PEACE OF MIND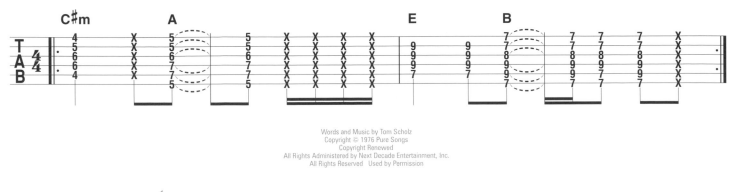

Boston's Tom Scholz is famous for creating a wall of sound, due not only to his production skills but also to his use of barre chords. Watch for the subtle alteration to the B chord in the second measure.

GET READY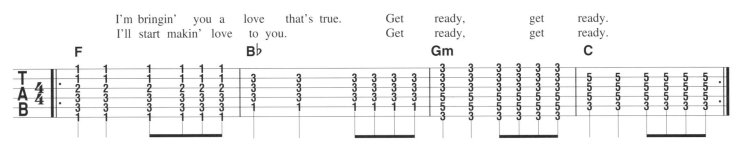

The chorus of this Rare Earth R&B classic is a barre chord-based progression.

LAYLA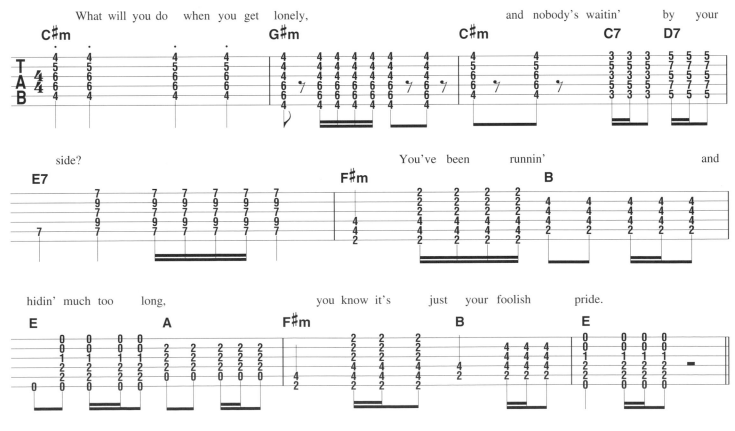

The main riff gets all the attention, but the verse progression is pretty nifty itself, as seen here. This also serves as an introduction to the A-shape dominant seventh barre chord, seen in measures 3 and 4. Notice how the shape resembles an open A7.

TIME IS ON MY SIDE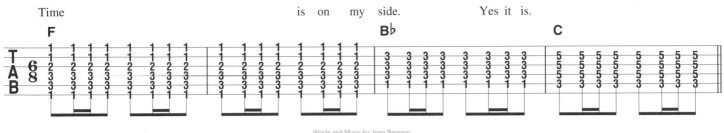

The Rolling Stones offered up a nice study in barre chords with this old hit in 6/8 time.

SHE'S WAITING

Eric Clapton's choice of a D minor chord offers a cool twist on this very popular progression that typically uses a D major chord in that spot.

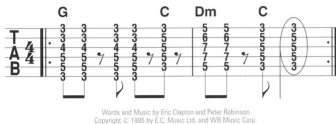

HERE I GO AGAIN

The chorus of this Whitesnake smash hit uses G, C, and D barre chords.

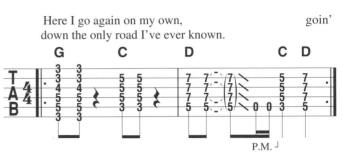

SOMEBODY TOLD ME

The Killers' 2003 "retro" smash features a barre-chord chorus section.

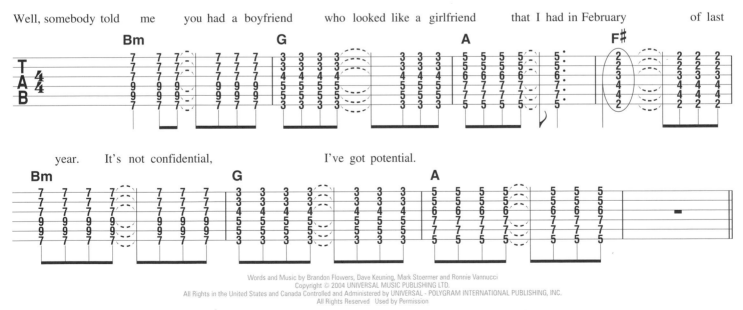

I CAN'T EXPLAIN

Rhythm guitar icon Pete Townshend got incredible mileage out of the simplest of chord riffs, as in this classic by the Who.

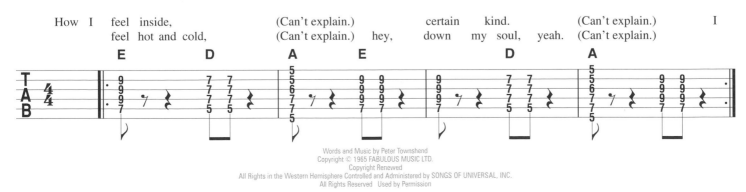

CHINA GROVE

Now that you've had some practice playing the four main types of barre chords, let's jam on this track by the Doobie Brothers.

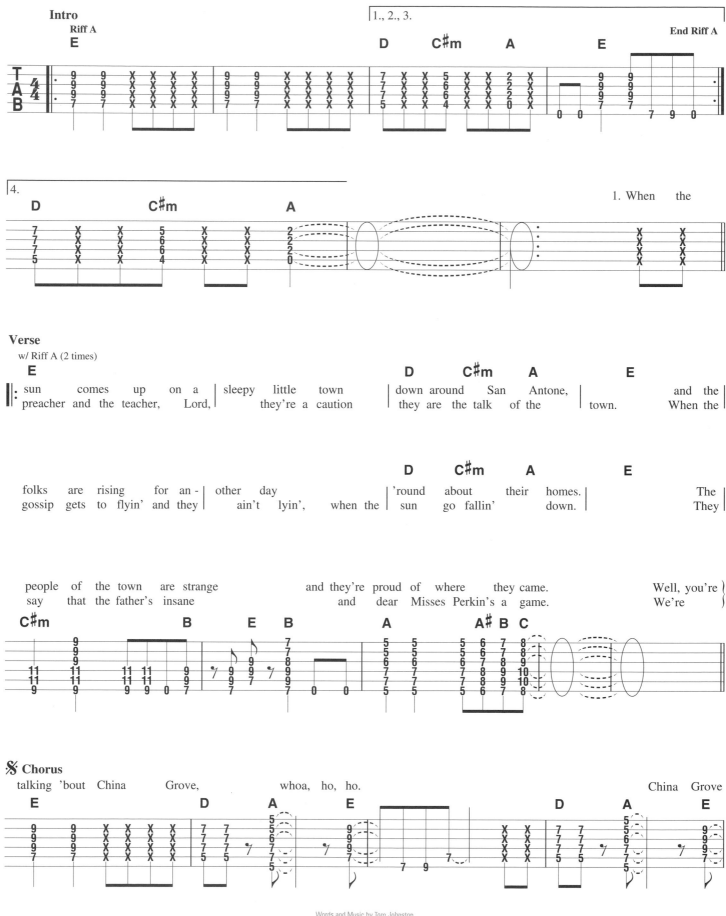

Words and Music by Tom Johnston
© 1973 (Renewed) WARNER-TAMERLANE PUBLISHING CORP.
All Rights Reserved Used by Permission

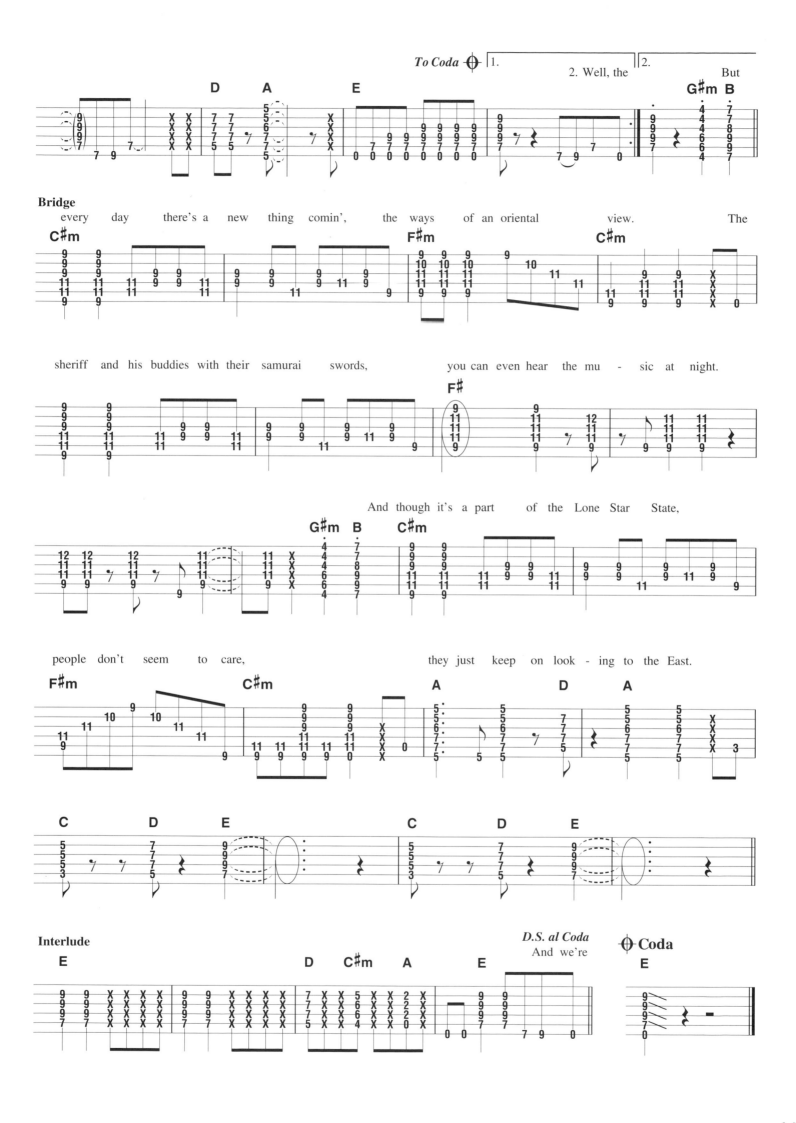

THE MINOR SCALE

Like the major scale, the **minor scale** also follows a specific pattern of whole steps and half steps. Here it is on the low E string.

E MINOR SCALE

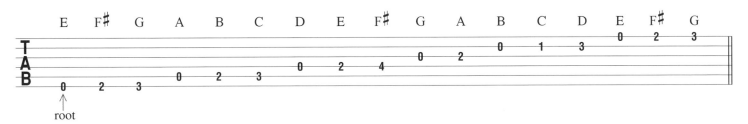

And like the major scale, the minor scale is most often played across several strings, not just along one string.

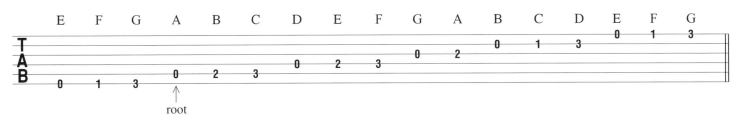

It's also very common to play a minor scale that has its root on the 5th string.

A MINOR SCALE

Naturally, both scales are movable; just find the root on the 6th or 5th string, place your index finger on it, and play the patterns shown in the diagrams below. Practice both scale patterns using alternate picking in both ascending and descending order.

Moveable Minor Scale – 6th-String Root

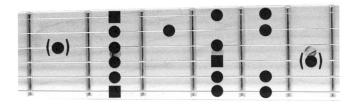

Moveable Minor Scale – 5th-String Root

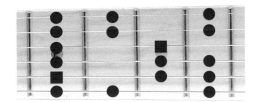

■ = root note

The notes of the minor scale form the foundation for countless rock riffs, licks, and solos. Here are just a few examples.

CRAZY TRAIN

Randy Rhoads expertly exploited the 6th-string-rooted minor scale pattern for this timeless riff.

MONEY

The 5th-string-rooted minor scale pattern is mined for Pink Floyd's "Money." Note the **7/4 time** signature—count seven quarter notes per measure.

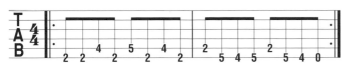

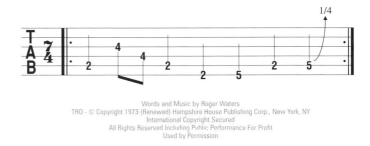

THE TROOPER

The signature riff of this Iron Maiden classic draws from the 5th-string-rooted E minor scale pattern and features a **trill**. Noted by the "tr" symbol in the notation, perform the trills by very rapidly alternating between the two adjacent notes (frets 7 and 8 on the 2nd string) using continuous hammer-ons and pull-offs.

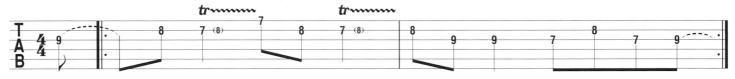

BREAKING THE LAW

An open-position A minor scale forms the foundation of this Judas Priest hit. Chord symbols are shown above the staff for reference.

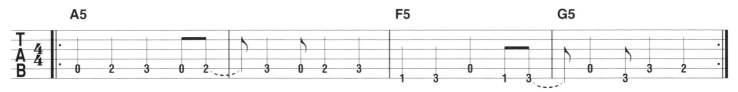

MR. CROWLEY

Guitarist Randy Rhoads played the interlude of Ozzy Osbourne's "Mr. Crowley" using the D minor scale. Chord symbols are included above the staff to show the harmony behind this melodic line.

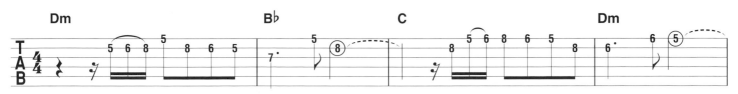

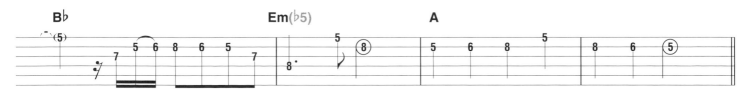

THE ZOO 🔊

For this shuffled Scorpions riff, diatonic 3rds in E minor are set against open low E notes. **Diatonic** means "notes belonging to the major or minor scale."

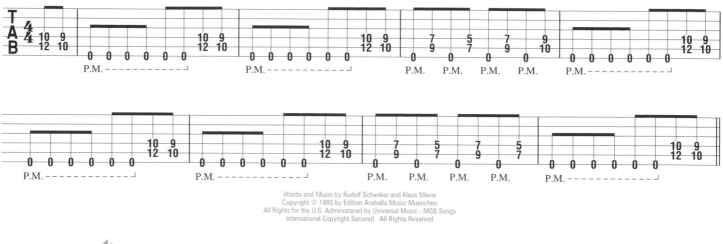

BEAT IT 🔊

This Michael Jackson megahit featured not only Eddie Van Halen on the guitar solo but also Steve Lukather cranking out the main riff in E minor.

IN MY DREAMS 🔊

George Lynch's giant riff in Dokken's "In My Dreams" comprises power chords carved from the E minor scale.

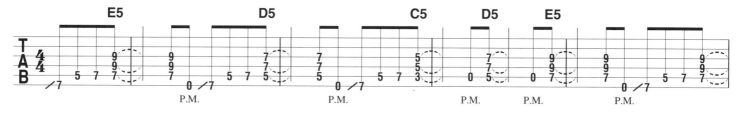

LAYLA 🔊

Eric Clapton's famous lead guitar riff uses notes from the D minor scale.

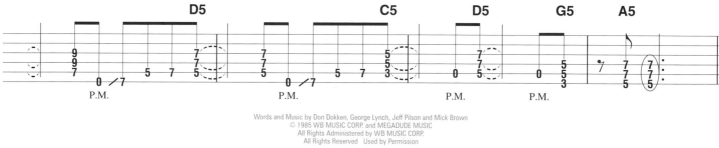

MUSIC THEORY 201

RELATIVE MINOR

Now that you've learned major and minor scales, let's take a look at a small but invaluable tidbit of music theory regarding these scales. Every major scale has a **relative minor scale** that contains the exact same notes, only you start on the 6th scale degree.

For example, a C major scale is spelled C–D–E–F–G–A–B.

If you play those exact same notes in the exact same order, but starting on the 6th degree, A, you'll play the A minor scale: A–B–C–D–E–F–G

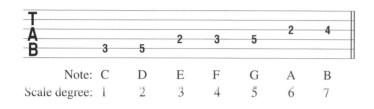

Note:	C	D	E	F	G	A	B
Scale degree:	1	2	3	4	5	6	7

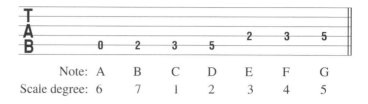

Note:	A	B	C	D	E	F	G
Scale degree:	6	7	1	2	3	4	5

Now here's the fun—and invaluable—part. To find the relative minor scale on the fretboard, all you need to do is slide down three frets from the major-scale root, and then play the minor scale. So, for example, if you're in the key of C, find the C note at the 8th fret on the 6th string. Then slide down three frets to the A note at the 5th fret and play the 6th-string root A minor scale pattern.

C Major and A Minor Patterns

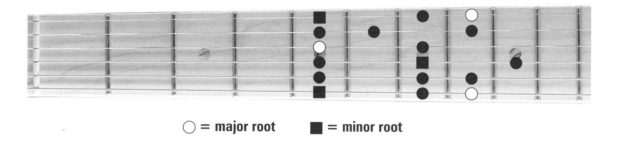

○ = major root ■ = minor root

Why is this invaluable? Because it helps you cover more of the fretboard when soloing. For example, if you're playing a song in the key of G major, you can play your solo using the G major scale and the relative E minor scale.

CHORD NUMBERS

In Book Two, you saw the notes of the C major scale assigned numbers, or degrees. Similarly, the chords found within a given key are not only determined by the major scale but are also assigned numbers. For example, take a look at the following chart. In the bottom row, you'll see Roman numerals assigned to each chord—uppercase indicates a major chord, lowercase a minor chord.

Major scale =	C	D	E	F	G	A	B
Diatonic chords =	C	Dm	Em	F	G	Am	B°
Chord numbers =	i	ii	iii	IV	V	vi	vii

This number system—sometimes called the **Nashville system**—is a shorthand method for labeling chords independent of key. For example, a I–vi–IV–V progression in the key of C contains the C, Am, F, and G chords, whereas a I–vi–IV–V in the key of A would contain A, F#m, D, and E chords.

12-BAR BLUES

The **12-bar blues** form is arguably the most important song form every guitarist must know. Consisting of 12 measures, or **bars**, it contains three chords—the I, IV, and V chords (typically dominant sevenths)—played in a specific order. Here's a sample 12-bar blues chart in the key of A. Play through it with the dominant seventh barre chords shown above the staff. The **slashes** (/) represent the four beats within each bar.

12-BAR BLUES – STANDARD FORM

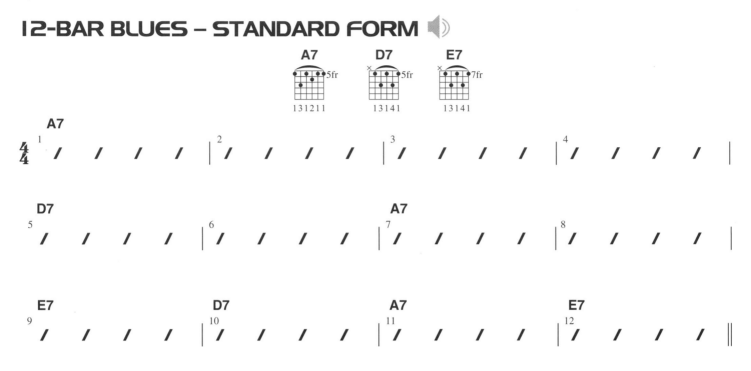

Another popular form of the 12-bar blues is called the **quick change**, which is identical to the standard form, except that you play the IV chord in bar 2.

12-BAR BLUES – QUICK CHANGE

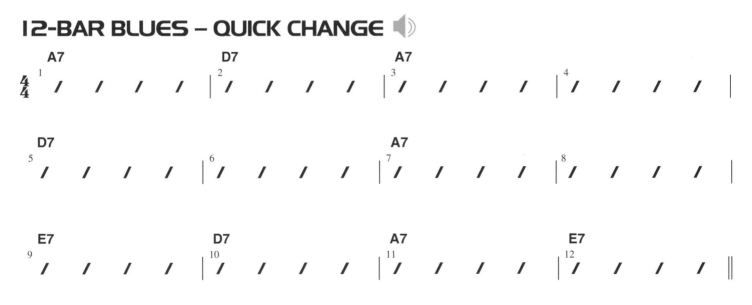

When improvising over a 12-bar blues, most guitarists use the **blues scale**, which is the same as the minor pentatonic, only with an added note—the ♭5th.

A BLUES SCALE

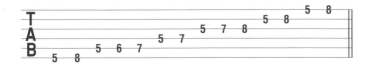

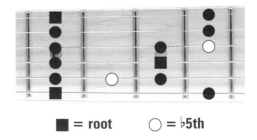

■ = root   ○ = ♭5th

From the blues scale, you can create blues licks. Here are several popular, "must-know" licks with tips on when to use them. Though these are shown in the key of A, they are all movable patterns. Also be sure to shuffle the eighth notes (long-short feel)— another vital element of blues.

BLUES LICK #1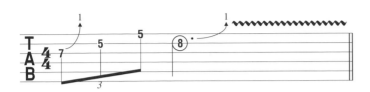

Use this lick over the I chord.

BLUES LICK #2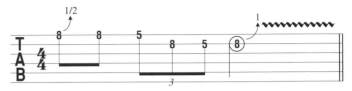

Use this one when moving from the IV to the I. Alternatively, play the first two beats as written but then land on the 7th-fret D (3rd string) when going from the I to the IV.

BLUES LICK #3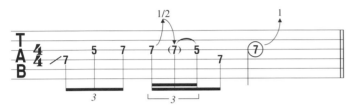

Use this one in bar 8, as a lead into the V chord. Notice the **sixteenth-note triplet**. Whereas an eighth-note triplet divides one beat into three parts, this divides one half of a beat into three parts.

BLUES LICK #4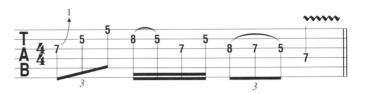

Use this lick over a I chord or in bar 10, to lead back to the I chord in bar 11.

In addition to the guitar solo, blues guitarists often use licks to fill in after a vocal line. This is called **call and response**, where the vocalist sings the "call," and the guitarist offers a "response." Freddie King's "I'm Tore Down" (popularly covered by Eric Clapton) offers a great example of this.

I'M TORE DOWN

Medium Shuffle

I'm tore down.   I'm almost   level with the ground.

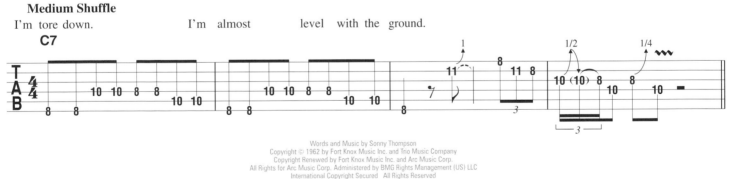

Another crucial component of blues is the **turnaround**. Because there are just 12 bars in the form, it is repeated over and over again, so the turnaround is used over the final two bars to signify that it's time to return to the top of the form.

TURNAROUND #1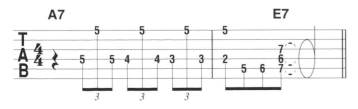

This one is for a shuffle blues in A. Use your pick on the 4th string and either your middle or ring finger to pluck the 1st string—a technique known as **hybrid picking**.

TURNAROUND #2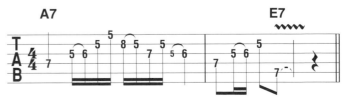

A standard "lick" that ends on the root of the V chord can also serve as a turnaround, like this one that is similar to what Eric Clapton played in Cream's "Crossroads."

SWEET HOME CHICAGO

Delta blues guitarist Robert Johnson is widely regarded as the most important artist in blues history. Of his 29 songs, "Sweet Home Chicago" is the most covered and has become a blues standard. Here's a modern arrangement you might hear at a local blues jam. There's a new chord type used in this song, the **ninth chord**, which is a "jazzy" substitute for a seventh chord. Note the four-bar intro and later the **stop-time** section, where the whole band stops while the vocalist sings the verses. These are two very popular blues devices.

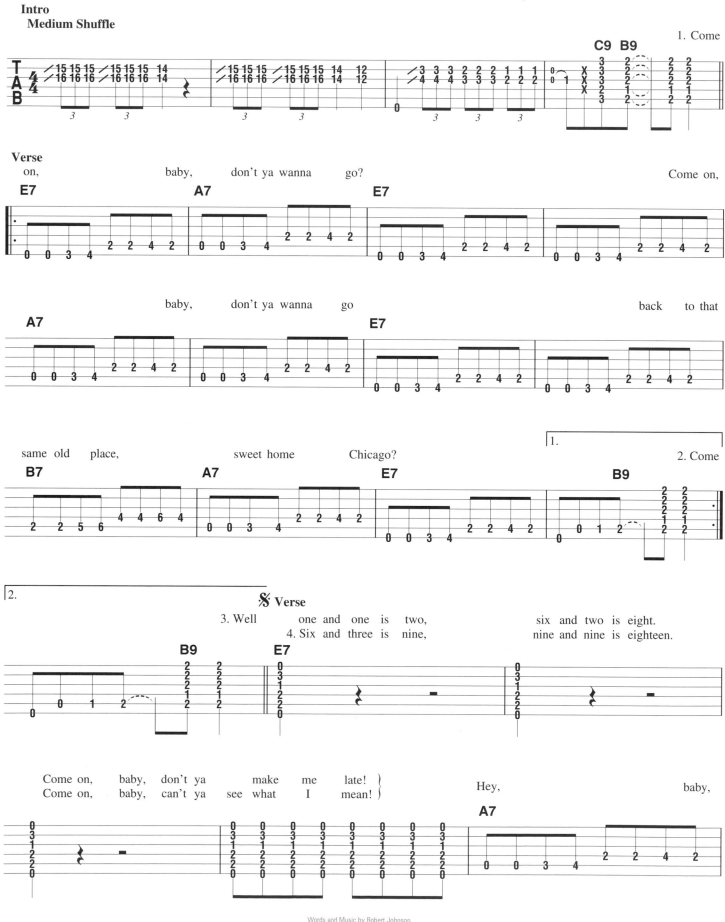

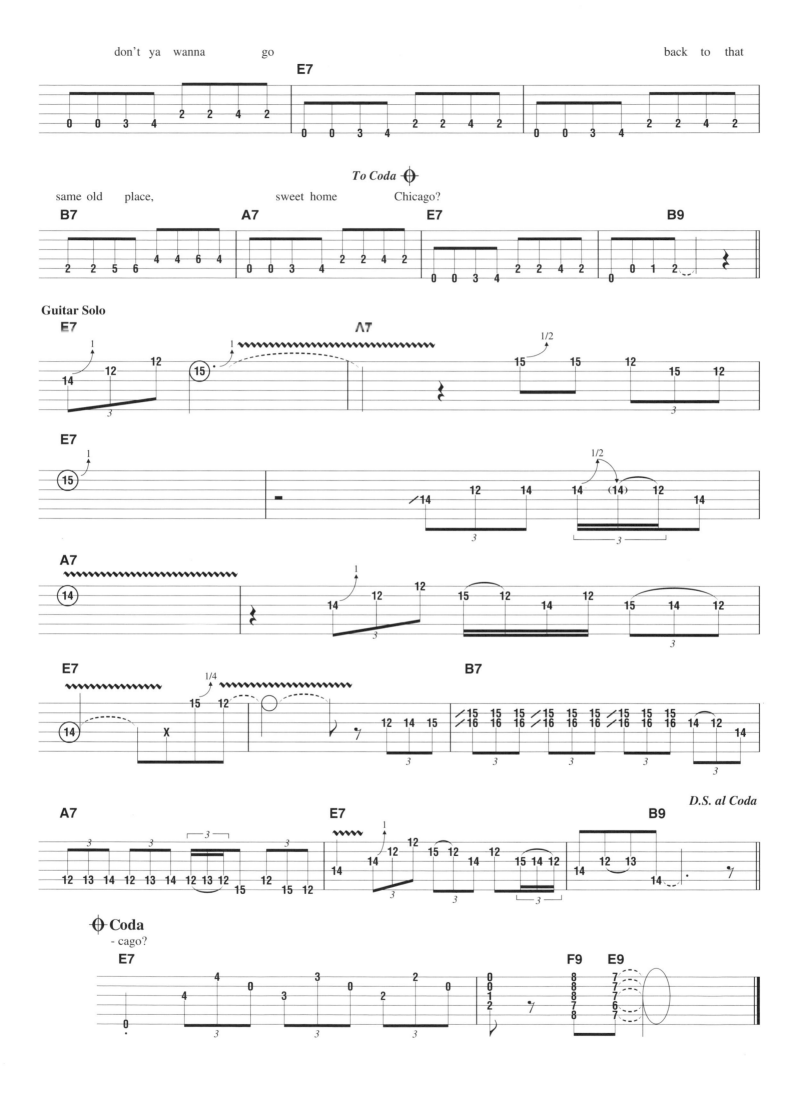

12/8 TIME

Some blues—particularly **slow blues**—are played in the alternate time signature of 12/8. This triplet-based compound meter is well suited for the blues and its attendant shuffle feel, and is very similar to 6/8 time (covered in Book Two).

In 12/8 time, each beat receives three eighth notes, and it is typically counted "**1**–2–3, **2**–2–3, **3**–2–3, **4**–2–3."

TEXAS FLOOD

Here's the 12/8 intro riff to Stevie Ray Vaughan's famous blues.

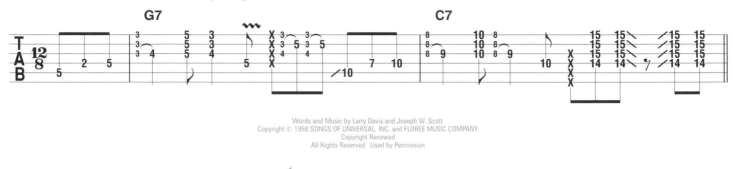

I CAN'T QUIT YOU BABY

The Willie Dixon-penned "I Can't Quit You Baby" is a 12/8 slow blues most famously performed by Otis Rush (shown here) and Led Zeppelin.

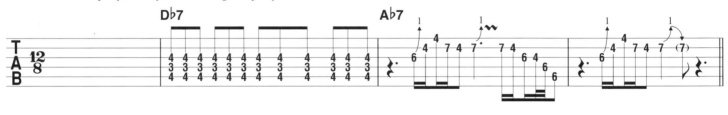

Blues isn't the only genre to use the 12/8 time signature. Many rock and pop artists have also used the rhythmic feel to great effect.

HOLD THE LINE

This Toto hit starts with a keyboard hitting every eighth note before Steve Lukather kicks on the overdrive for this great riff.

MISUNDERSTANDING

Genesis showed how a really simple riff can be made interesting using the 12/8 time signature.

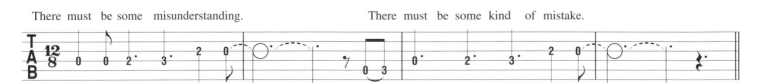

(THEY CALL IT) STORMY MONDAY

Perhaps the most famous 12/8 blues ever written, artists including B.B. King, Kenny Burrell, Leslie West, and the Allman Brothers Band have covered this T-Bone Walker classic. Yet another option for movable seventh chords is given at the start of the song. Notice how this shape resembles the C7 chord you learned in Book Two.

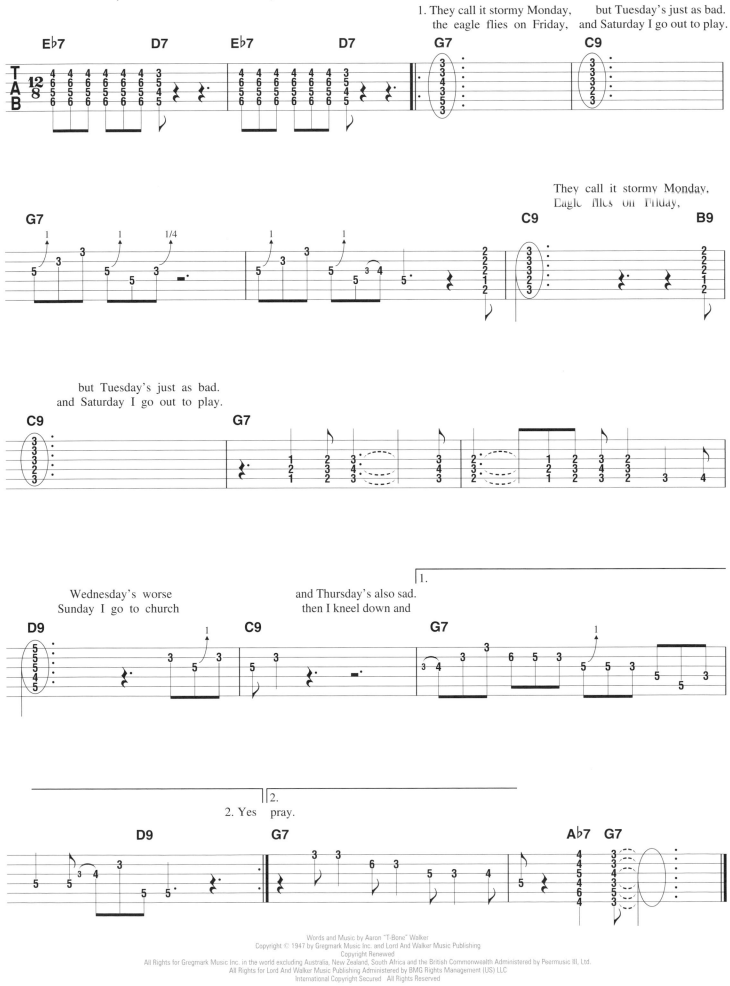

ADD & SUS CHORDS

Major and minor chords (or **triads**) comprise three notes—the root, 3rd, and 5th (major) and the root, ♭3rd, and 5th (minor). In this section, we're going to show you how to alter these triads either by addition or by substitution.

ADD CHORDS

An **add** chord is just what it sounds like—a triad with a fourth note added to it. Typically, the 2nd (or 9th) note of the chord's attendant scale is the added note, with the 4th (or 11th) also occasionally used.

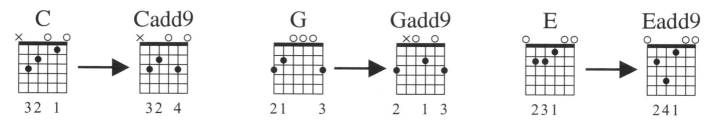

Probably the most popular add chord is the Cadd9 in this alternative form, typically following or preceding a G chord.

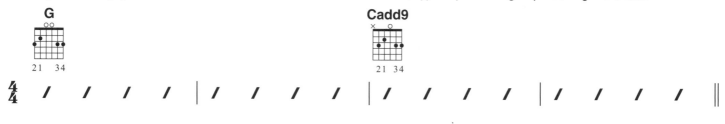

3 AM 🔊

"3 AM," which epitomizes the G–Cadd9 progression, was a huge hit for modern rockers Matchbox 20 in the mid-'90s.

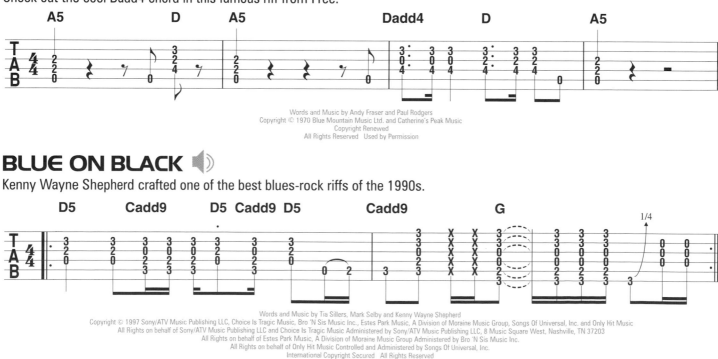

ALL RIGHT NOW 🔊

Check out the cool Dadd4 chord in this famous riff from Free.

BLUE ON BLACK 🔊

Kenny Wayne Shepherd crafted one of the best blues-rock riffs of the 1990s.

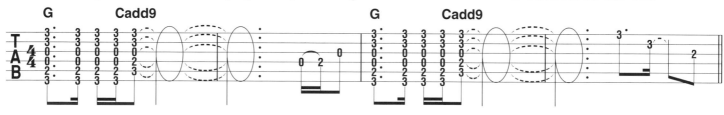

SUS CHORDS

In a triad, the 3rd degree determines whether it's major or minor in **tonality** (or quality). So if you remove the 3rd degree and instead play the 2nd or 4th in its place, you "suspend" the chord's tonality. This is called a **sus** chord.

The most common sus chords are built on open D and A chords.

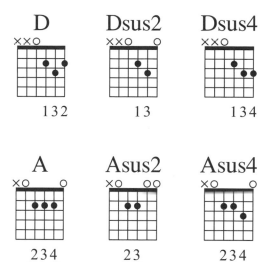

ZIGGY STARDUST

In this David Bowie classic, guitarist Mick Ronson implies alternating D and Dsus4 chords in bar 1, then employs some nice voice leading via a descending bass line beginning on Cadd9 and ending on Gsus2 (with the suspended A in the bass).

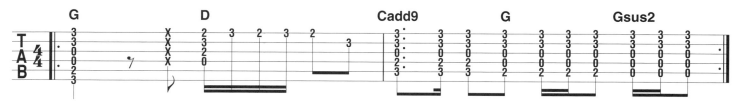

SUMMER OF '69

The arpeggio riff in this Bryan Adams hit cycles through both D and A triads and their related sus2 and sus4 chords.

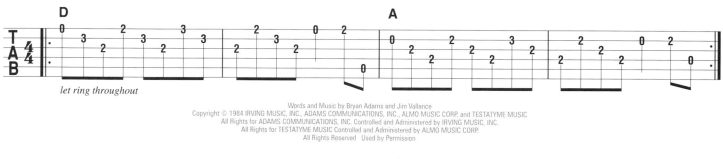

JAMES TAYLOR SIGNATURE LICK

Acoustic singer-songwriter James Taylor calls this sus chord move, heard in "Fire and Rain," "Sweet Baby James," and "Carolina on My Mind," among others, one of his "pet licks."

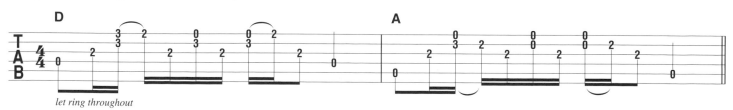

SUS2 BARRE CHORDS

By far, the most common sus2 barre chord is the movable version of the open Asus2.

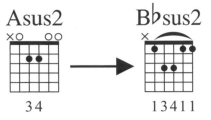

ROCKSTAR

Check out the chorus to this huge 2005 hit from Nickelback.

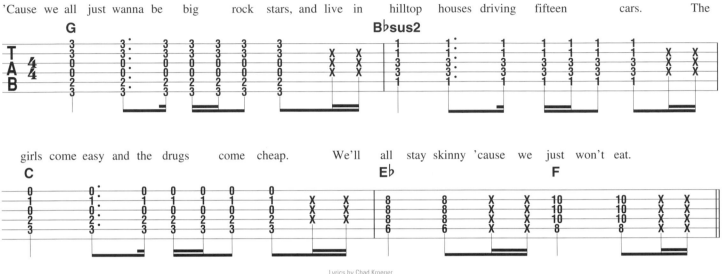

Lyrics by Chad Kroeger
Music by Nickelback
© 2005 WARNER-TAMERLANE PUBLISHING CORP., ARM YOUR DILLO PUBLISHING INC., ZERO-G MUSIC, INC., BLACK DIESEL MUSIC, INC. and DANIEL ADAIR PUBLISHING DESIGNEE
All Rights Administered by WARNER-TAMERLANE PUBLISHING CORP.
All Rights Reserved   Used by Permission

LIGHTNING CRASHES

Live's 1994 hit thundered across the airwaves on its way to becoming an alt-rock standard.

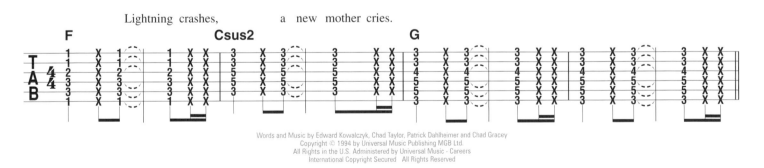

Words and Music by Edward Kowalczyk, Chad Taylor, Patrick Dahlheimer and Chad Gracey
Copyright © 1994 by Universal Music Publishing MGB Ltd.
All Rights in the U.S. Administered by Universal Music - Careers
International Copyright Secured   All Rights Reserved

NATURAL SCIENCE

The movable sus2 chord is especially popular in progressive rock, a style that thrives on ambiguous major-minor tonality. No prog-rock guitarist has gotten more mileage from this chord than Rush's Alex Lifeson, as epitomized by this fan favorite from their 1980 release *Permanent Waves*.

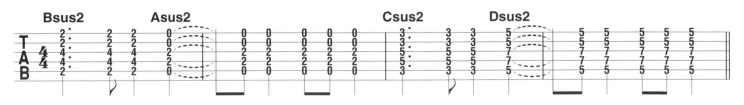

Words by Neil Peart
Music by Geddy Lee, Alex Lifeson and Neil Peart
© 1980 CORE MUSIC PUBLISHING
All Rights Reserved   Used by Permission

Another highly popular form of the sus2 chord is the movable arpeggiated version in the root–5th–2nd voicing, with the root found on either the 6th or 5th string.

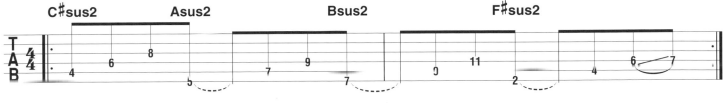

You might say Police guitarist Andy Summers has built a career on the sus2 chord—two of the band's biggest hits are based on it!

MESSAGE IN A BOTTLE

Here, Summers simply moves the same shape around the neck to create one of the greatest rock riffs of all time.

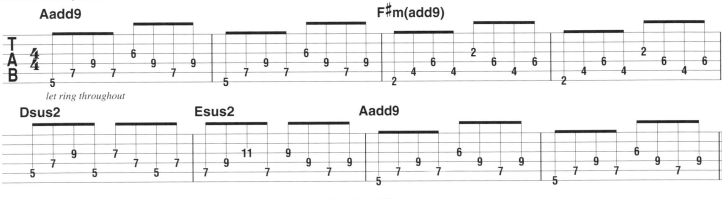

EVERY BREATH YOU TAKE

In this ballad, Summers mixes add and sus chords.

SUS4 BARRE CHORDS

The sus4 version of the movable A-shape barre chord is the most popular voicing, and nearly always resolves to its major triad.

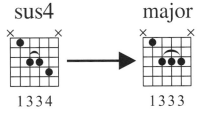

UNCHAINED

Guitar legend Eddie Van Halen put the suspended 4th on the heavy metal map with this classic riff. For this song, you'll need to be in **drop D tuning**; tune your 6th string down one whole step to D.

*Drop D tuning

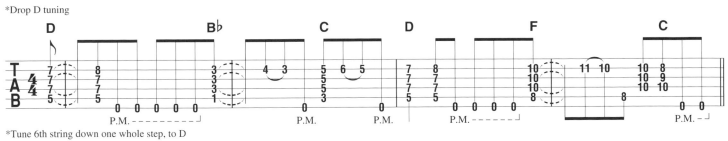

*Tune 6th string down one whole step, to D

WANTED DEAD OR ALIVE

Bon Jovi was the biggest rock band on the planet in the mid-1980s, thanks in part to this smash hit that includes add and sus chords. The guitar solo features a new type of string bend called a **pre-bend**. Designated by a vertical arrow in the tab, first bend the string to pitch as indicated, and then strike it. Note that the original recording was played with a 12-string acoustic guitar.

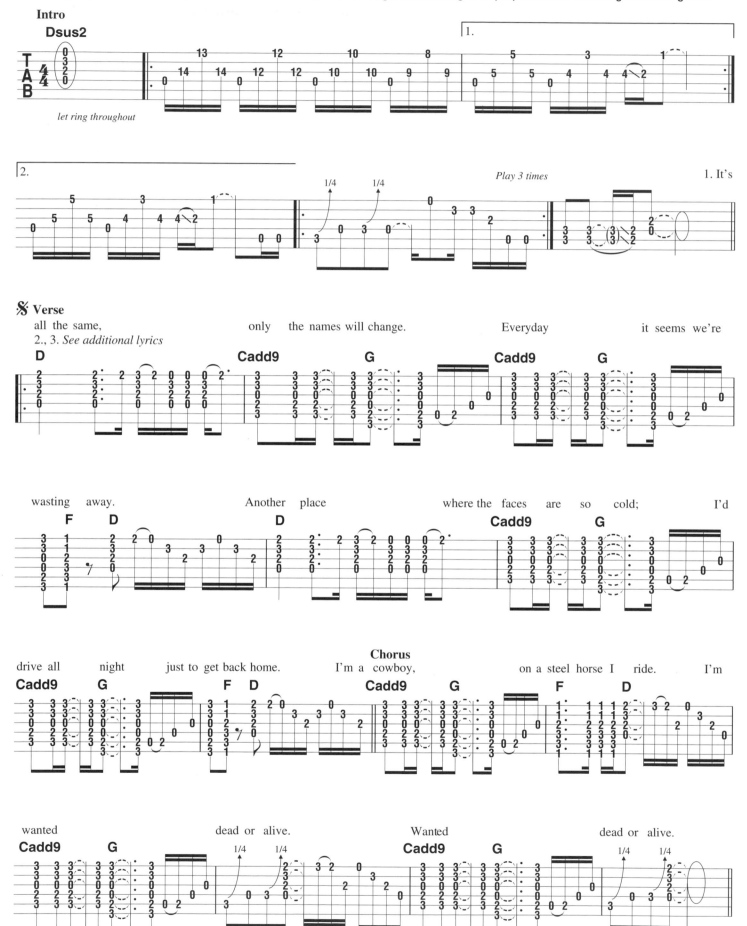

Interlude

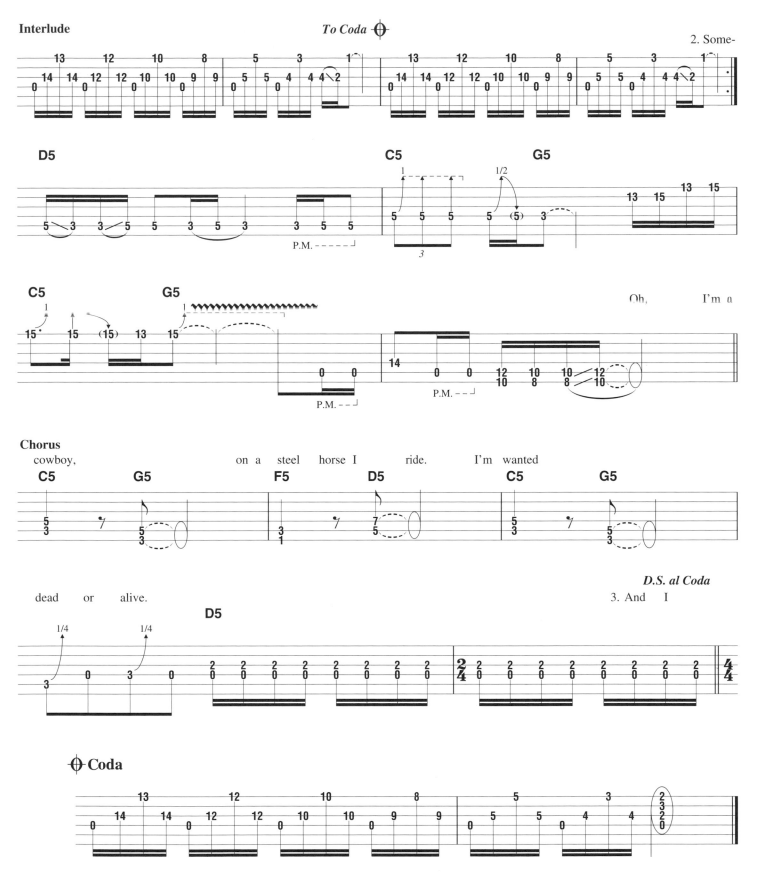

Additional Lyrics

2. Sometimes I sleep, sometimes it's not for days.
   The people I meet always go their sep'rate ways.
   Sometimes you tell the day by the bottle that you drink.
   And times when you're alone, all you do is think.

3. And I walk these streets, a loaded six-string on my back.
   I play for keeps, 'cause I might not make it back.
   I've been ev'rywhere, still I'm standing tall.
   I've seen a million faces and I've rocked them all.

MINOR SEVENTH CHORDS

You've already learned how to play dominant seventh chords in open position, so now let's take a look at their minor cousin. A **minor seventh** chord contains four notes: the root, ♭3rd, 5th, and ♭7th. In open position, you'll find Am7, Dm7, and Em7 chords, some with multiple fingering options.

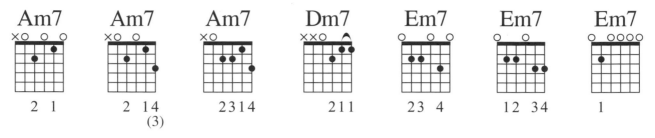

ROCKY RACCOON

Strum this Beatles classic with a shuffle feel (shuffled sixteenths). Notice there are few new chords and fingerings. The last chord is a **slash chord**, called C/B (pronounced "C over B"), in which the note to the right of the slash is the bass note of the chord—in this case, it's a C chord with a B in the bass.

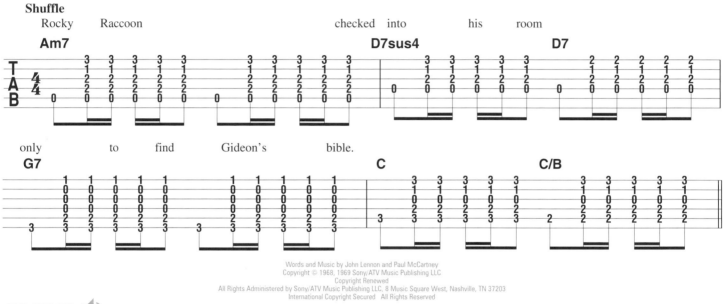

OURS

This Taylor Swift hit uses a combination of triads, minor sevenths, and add9 chords all featuring the same three notes, or **common tones**, on the top three strings. Note that Swift plays these chord shapes with a **capo**—a device that clamps across all six strings at a given fret, to change the song's key—at the 5th fret.

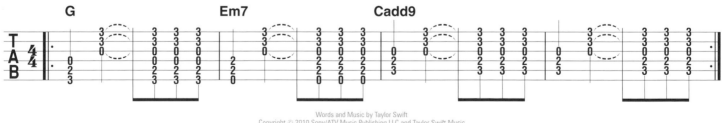

CRUISE

Florida-Georgia Line hit the country-rock charts in 2013 with their first hit, "Cruise."

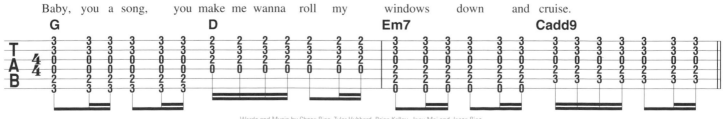

MINOR SEVENTH BARRE CHORDS

There are two main barre chord forms of the minor seventh chord: one with a 6th-string root and one with a 5th-string root.

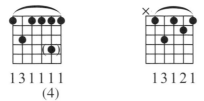

LIGHTS

Journey guitarist Neal Schon used arpeggiated chords to craft this timeless rock riff in 6/8 time.

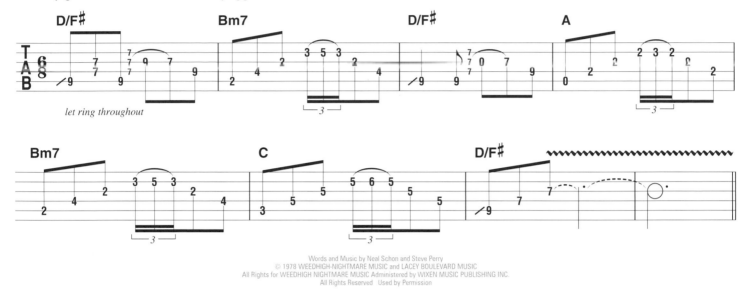

THIS LOVE

"This Love" was Maroon 5's breakthrough hit back in 2002, due in equal parts to its syncopated intro riff and the catchy chorus shown here.

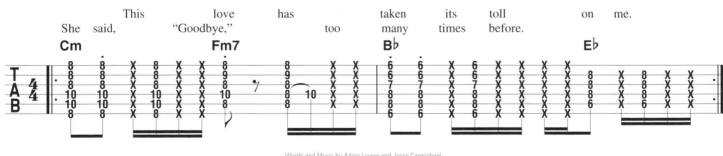

LONG TRAIN RUNNIN'

This famous riff from the Doobie Brothers puts a twist on the minor seventh chord, requiring you to barre all six strings to create a Gm11 chord (an extended version of Gm7), and then hammering onto the 2nd and 4th strings to create the Gm7 chord.

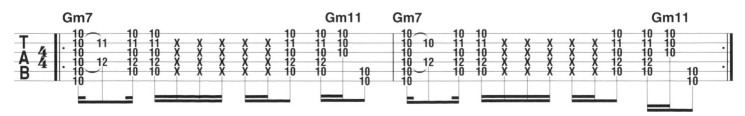

MINOR BLUES

Earlier, you learned about the 12-bar blues form using dominant seventh chords, but you can also use minor seventh chords, which results in a **minor blues**. The minor blues form is essentially the same as the standard one, except you play minor seventh chords in place of the I and IV chords. The V chord, however, sometimes remains dominant. Here's a sample minor blues form.

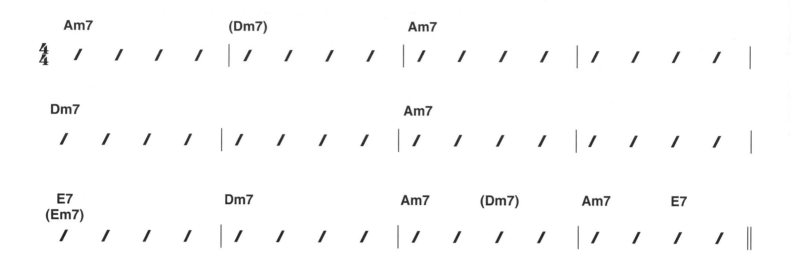

ALL YOUR LOVE (I MISS LOVING)

This Otis Rush classic, famously covered by the Bluesbreakers with Eric Clapton, contains one of the most famous minor blues interludes ever recorded. But instead of full minor seventh chords, it features mostly arpeggiated minor triads.

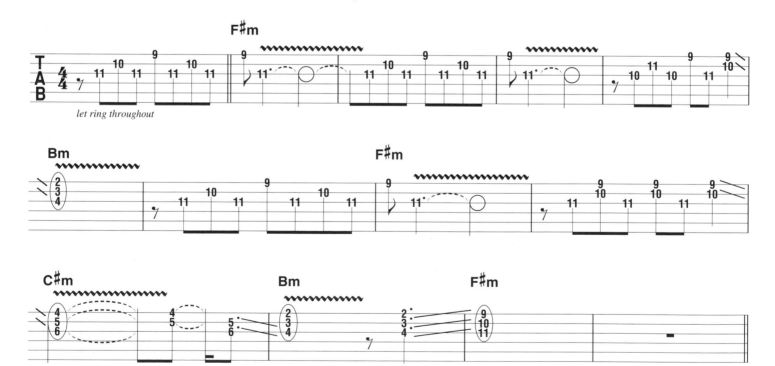

Words and Music by Otis Rush
Copyright © 1965 (Renewed) by Conrad Music, a division of Arc Music Corp. (BMI)
All Rights Administered by BMG Rights Management (US) LLC
International Copyright Secured   All Rights Reserved
Used by Permission

BLACK MAGIC WOMAN 🔊

Peter Green, guitarist in the original British blues incarnation of Fleetwood Mac, wrote this 1969 minor blues classic. Carlos Santana then famously covered it a year later on his 1970 release *Abraxas*. Here is Santana's iconic intro solo.

UNDER THE BRIDGE

Let's close out Book Three with this huge hit by the Red Hot Chili Peppers. The condensed arrangement features the intro, verse, pre-chorus, and bridge guitar parts, including two new chord shapes: the opening D and the verse's Emaj7. Fret the D chord with your fingers 4, 3, 1, and 2 on strings 5, 4, 3, and 2, respectively.

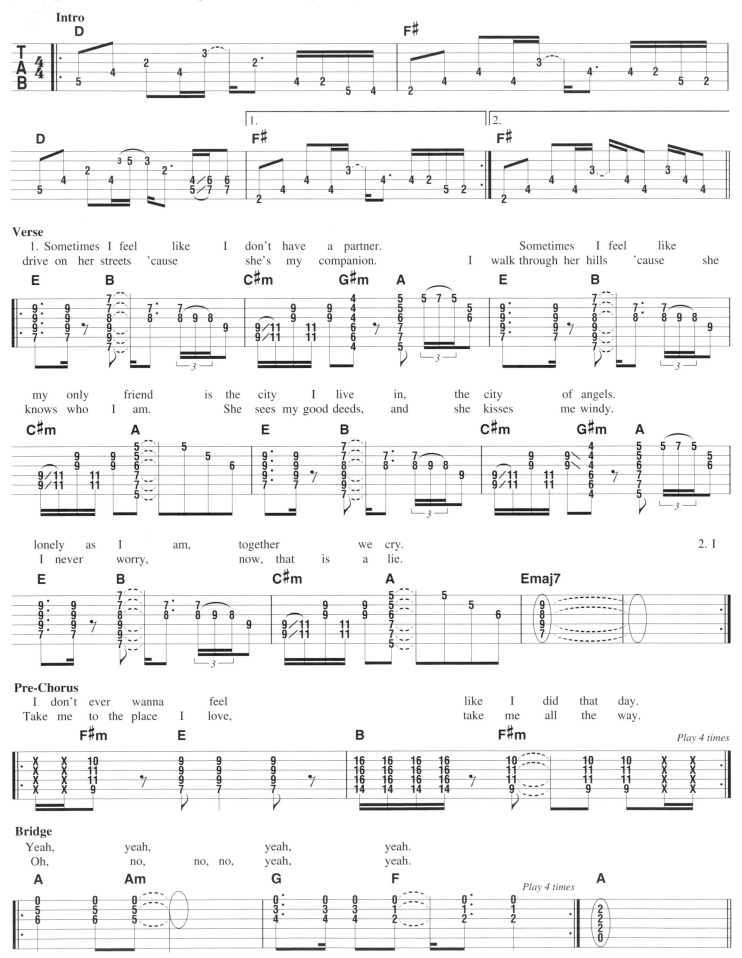

Words and Music by Anthony Kiedis, Flea, John Frusciante and Chad Smith
© 1991 MOEBETOBLAME MUSIC
All Rights Reserved   Used by Permission